This is our story of love, life
that comes from a cancer diag

Our Oesophageal Cancer Journey From A Wife's Perspective

Written By
Sarah Keyworth

I have written this book to help me make sense of this living nightmare but also in the hope that in some small way, it may help some of you realise that you are not alone, you are not going mad, it really can happen to anyone but most importantly, you can and will get through it. I am not a writer so forgive me for the candid way it is written with the odd swear word and probably far from perfect grammar but it is real and written from the heart, that I can assure you.

I have been in a relationship with Graham for 26 years and married for 22. We have worked abroad together, ran pubs together, in fact done most things together. Graham is 61 and very healthy, has never smoked, does a heavy manual job and he is very rarely ill. I have known him be poorly twice in all those years so when he said to me that food feels like it is sticking a bit, I thought nothing of it. Maybe he has just got a sore throat, maybe his glands are up, maybe his one and only health condition which is a sliding hernia is playing him up but I suggested to call the doctors just to be sure suspecting that they would probably just change his medication from Omeprazole to an alternative. Then one night we had an incident that frightened the life out of me when food actually got stuck and he started choking, this was alarm bells and clearly not normal so he called the GP who immediately said we will refer you for an endoscopy just to rule out gullet cancer.

Why would he say that C word? What has that got to do with us?

Why do they just bat that bloody word around like it is no big deal? Why do they worry you when there is no way it can be cancer? Cancer would never happen to us…

On Wednesday 10th May 2023, Graham had his appointment for an endoscopy which was performed by Di, a great friend of ours that we have known for nearly 20 years. He didn't have sedation so it was just a case of nipping in, having it done and then back home with no recovery time from the sedative. I don't need to go in with him as she is just going to say it is just your hernia so I pop off to Tesco in my own little happy world and then make my way back to the hospital.
A friend had given us a lift so we were sitting chatting in the car when I received a text message from Graham ….
Can you come up to endoscopy, nothing to worry about, they just want to talk about what happens next. Why does he need me to go in and meet him, he can listen to what is next because it will only be a change of medication or diet. Ok I understand that you want me there in case you miss anything they say so that's ok I think……… hang on why is there a lump in my throat? Why can I not breathe properly? What is this feeling of dread? Oh for gods sake Sarah, sort yourself out, it is just a change of diet or meds. Why was I feeling so nervous?

I made my way to the endoscopy department physically shaking and was told to sit in the waiting room until I was called in. It seemed like an eternity but realistically was only 5 minutes until my name was called and I was shown into 'that' room.
Di who was looking straight faced and calm along with another calm looking lady (who is now our gastrointestinal nurse Becky)

and Graham were sitting around a table and that was the moment I knew our lives were about to change forever. The first words I heard were I am so very sorry but we have found something, suspicious, tumour, 8 biopsies, tests, scans, ultrasound, oesophageal cancer….. WAIT WHAT did you say CANCER ? I said to our friend do you mean it may be cancer and she said no, it is definitely cancer I'm afraid. I am sure time stood still and I watched our world explode into pieces right before my eyes. We were told that there will be a plan and as soon as all testing is complete, then they will know exactly what they are dealing with and how to tackle this. Di walked downstairs with us as we sort of stumbled along in utter disbelief. She gave us both a big hug and said we will support you all the way with this, there will be options. Trust the process.

Well that was a numb walk out of the hospital, into our friends car and all the way home. I didn't know what to do or say, I didn't know what to think, I didn't know what Graham was thinking but I knew our world was crashing down and life would never be the same, we would never be the same. Then it sunk in, my husband/soul mate/best friend has cancer so I sobbed and sobbed which upset Graham and then he said right, come on get a grip. I am not going anywhere, I WILL fight and beat this so don't worry. Don't worry? Are you fucking mad, you've got cancer ! It's ok, he said. One test at a time, one day at a time. We will be ok. He seemed to completely accept it with no question and said it is ok, they will come up with a plan that will work and get rid of it. How can he be so sure? But he was sure and his attitude was amazing, I felt so utterly crushed and he was totally accepting of the situation. God he is a strong man and I need to take a leaf out of his book.

Ok what can I do to help us start this battle. I went and purchased some Complan to help boost him up and get some good stuff in him, I know his eating will probably get worse now we know that he has a tumour growing that will restrict his oesophagus even further so a liquid supplement will start us off on a good footing. I need to be strong and supportive and I need life to carry on without constantly talking about cancer because he is still Graham so I must not treat him any differently to usual. It is too easy to constantly say how do you feel, can you swallow that, is everything ok. While he was at work and coping with amazing strength and determination with this thing growing. I googled ...... that is it, he won't last 5 years, will be lucky for him to last 2, palliative care only, stage 4, no hope, not a good cancer to have, fuck me, name me a good one! DO NOT GOOGLE, DR GOOGLE IS NOT YOUR FRIEND. I know you will because that is what we do but remember that a lot of the statistics are outdated, a lot are just averages and a lot are different treatments to what you will have. Each story is different and unique so you are your own statistic. Another thing I found was instead of googling oesophageal cancer survival times, if you MUST research, try Oesophageal cancer success stories and you will feel a lot better than reading a lot of the bad.

Right, I must be strong for him. No crying or breaking down as it will upset him. Keep it together, keep it together, you have to keep it together for him. Graham was carrying on as though nothing had happened, going to work and being his normal self. Was it denial?
I don't think so, I really think it was acceptance.

A meeting was called with Dr Mathews at the hospital the week after the biopsies were taken so our fate will be sealed and we will know exactly what we are up against. It's a peculiar feeling knowing that you have cancer is one bombshell but now it is a case of how bad is it, is it treatable. With numb fear on my part we went off to see what we had in store. We sat in the waiting room with my head full of palliative care only, get your affairs in order, it will be a matter of months not years, very sorry but there is nothing we can do. Graham was as cool as a cucumber, I mean really. He wasn't being brave because he knew I was a mess, he really was very calm. I took a notepad and pen in so I could be practical and write key words down and give me something to focus on. I never really knew what utter desperation and sheer fear felt like up until that moment. I felt sick, shaky, nervous and faint with a feeling of impending doom.

We walked into his room and was greeted by a lovely man who introduced himself in the most calming voice, he had such a lovely demeanour about him. I guess if you have to give people devastating news, you either become desensitised or you become compassionate and he was definitely the latter. The meeting was a blur to be honest but the words that stuck were Small, caught early, hopeful, treatment, operation, chemo, radiotherapy, trials, immunotherapy, hope.
He said it was Squamous cell cancer but he has age and fitness on his side and he is in a good position for treatment.

Wait…… did he said SMALL, CAUGHT EARLY, TREATMENT? Yes he did, we have HOPE now and I'm not letting that bastard go.

It's funny how you can leave an appointment knowing your loved one has cancer but actually feeling happy because we have hope.

Ok let us be practical, what comes next, what do we need to do?. Boost his food and help him maintain his weight, get nutritional supplement shakes from the dietitian at the hospital, CT Scan, PET Scan, Endoscopic Ultrasound, Staging Laparoscopy op. A whirlwind of things to do, appointments to book, lifestyle changes and god knows what else to think about all whilst trying to have a 'normal' life. I started researching diets for people fighting cancer and what was good or bad for him to eat. I don't need to worry about strength building because Graham has a very physical job and is already extremely fit at the moment but I need to keep his protein up and not let the cancer eat away at him physically. It is now that I keep thinking that surely the tumour is growing each day without treatment so isn't time critical? We may be ok at the minute because it was caught early but by the time all the testing is completed, he could be terminal. Why do these thoughts get into your head? Why do I keep feeling the worse?

First on the testing schedule was the CT scan which is the doughnut machine with contrast dye to help show if the cancer is spreading beyond the oesophagus. When I had a CT a few years ago, I found out the hard way that I was allergic to the contrast dye so I was hoping that Graham wouldn't be the same.
The results will be discussed at a weekly meeting and we will find out once all staging tests are completed. Graham was focused and faced it all with ease and no problems having it done.

Next was the staging laparoscopy operation to help with the staging of the cancer. It was heartbreaking leaving him in the surgical short stay unit on his own knowing that he was being put to sleep for the first time in our lives. We had absolutely no idea that part of staging cancer would involve an operation. We had to be at the hospital for 7.30am and Graham was due to go down early so they told me to call at lunchtime to arrange picking him up. That was a day of feeling sick, numb, terrified and nervous. I called at lunchtime and they said he hadn't gone down yet as there was a complication with the operation before him but it won't be long, the poor bugger didn't even have his phone with him as they said not to bring in anything valuable. The call came at roughly 5.30pm to say 'he has eaten and had a drink, as soon as he has had a pee you can collect him'. Yay, he is coming home! A neat cut in his belly button and one above to the left, all glued together as though nothing had happened. The results, again will be about 2 weeks or so. The surgeon came around while we were waiting for his cannulas to be taken out and said he was very happy with how it went. He now has no lifting more than a kilo for 4 weeks and no driving for 2 weeks and lots of rest. So the healing and building up began. He coped very well with it and recovered quickly bouncing back to being himself with that great positive attitude, he had some shoulder pain which the nurse explained to us that it is trapped wind and perfectly normal, she said to try to walk around as much as he can and drink warm drinks which will help the wind get out which it did. We had some lovely days sitting in the garden while he healed and he soon went back to work on light duties by driving a mate around who did all the lifting while Graham chauffeured.

We also found out during a routine ECG at his pre op assessment for the laparoscopy that Graham has left bundle branch block in his heart which we never knew about but they do not seem too concerned about that as he has no symptoms, so I am skipping past that because I cannot focus or Google the negative effects and go back to that dark place in my head. Must keep it together for him, remember.

Within a week of the laparoscopy was the PET scan, Graham got injected with radioactive dye and had to lie in a room for an hour while the dye spread throughout his body before another trip through the magic all seeing doughnut. As usual he breezed through it with positivity as though it was just routine and normal to be having it done. It seems part of our weekly routine now to pack him off to the hospital. Please don't think I am heartless by not going to some of these appointments, Graham said there is no point if it just tests without results and the departments do get busy in the waiting areas.

Next on the whistle stop tour was the EUS which is an endoscopic ultrasound that had to be done under sedation because it would otherwise be too painful and allows them to have a good root around. This all helps along with the other tests to stage and show any spread and show the exact position and size of the tumour. I was called in after the endoscopy had been done and Graham was ready to be collected.

We were told that it went well and the nurse said those words that we had heard before SMALL, CAUGHT EARLY, TREATMENT. She said get yourself as fit and healthy as you can for the big operation. So it sounds like they are hopeful of it being operable.

It was quite funny going into the room to collect him as he was so dopey from the sedation bless him but still his happy jokey self. We then had a chat with our dietitian who went through what Graham was eating to ensure he was getting enough calories and to ask us if we had any concerns.

All of these tests now go to the big oncology meeting which are held every Tuesday morning for our team to discuss and work out the best plan of attack. So while we try to have some sort of life, his fate is in the hands of a team of experts chatting over coffee. We have a fantastic hospital and I have no doubt that he is in expert hands but it is still very surreal thinking that his life is now under their control. What they say, goes. It is a fantastic job that they all do and it must be so hard for them when they build up a relationship with you only to look at results and know there is nothing they can do but on the same token, it's must be a great feeling looking and thinking we can save this one.

It is now Saturday the 17th of June so all of this has happened in only 5 weeks. God bless our NHS!. Honestly, it annoys me when people moan about them. We have nothing but admiration for everyone we have met on our journey so far at The Royal Surrey Hospital in Guildford and the attached St Luke's. We have been treated with speed, compassion and really feel like they all care. We now have a few days of normality until we get called in to discuss the plan so for now it is high calorie foods little and often and trying to make mince and softer food exciting. I am already a master in small dicing and thinking of inventive things to do with easily swallowable food.

My advice is to encourage them to eat full fat things, drink full fat milk, eat whatever they fancy because we are at the start of a long hard battle. I add full fat milk powder to sweet things and bone broth powder to savoury dishes, extra butter in mashed potatoes with lots of cheese, I make ice cream with clotted cream and double cream, anything for extra calories. We have a great support network, our friends Don & Shirley have been rocks taking us to all of the hospital appointments and waiting around for hours just because they care, my friend Pari who has listened to me shout, cry, moan at her and has accepted it all without judgement and shown us nothing but support. Fundamentally though, it is us that closes the door behind us and have to realise that this is our new normal for a while.

Graham hasn't once felt sorry for himself, he is so determined and is just treating it as a little bump in the road, he was more worried about me! You are the one with cancer, stop worrying about me! But that just proves the type of husband he is. I have been through, why him?, anger, sadness, worry and utter despair in the last few weeks but the one thing I now know in my heart is that he WILL beat this, he will come out the other side and one day we will look back on this as one of life's obstacles while we eat a big juicy steak and celebrate. But for now, I am using Grahams mantra of one day at a time. I asked him if he is angry about it or scared or anything and he said no, it is just luck of the draw, it is just something that can happen to anyone and it has just happened to me. He said I am fine, I just have something in me that shouldn't be there but it will get sorted.

The call has come. Becky, our nurse has given us the heads up that Graham is going to have to have pre operative chemo along with a feeding tube and then an exercise test in preparation for the 'big' op so it sounds hopeful ! Actually it sounds like a 'buckle up, it's going to be a bumpy ride' but if it means he survives then bring it on. Hopefully we should hear in the next 3 days with dates …..

We have had a call to let us know that the pre op exercise test is now booked in for the 6th of July to make sure his heart and lungs can cope with the big operation because they have to collapse a lung for a big part of it. Oncology also want to see us on Monday 26th June so it is all starting to happen. I am truly praying that chemo is kind to Graham as I have heard so many bad stories but also so many good. I hope he doesn't lose his determination and keeps this fantastic fuck cancer attitude. If anyone can cope with treatment, it is going to be him. It is our 22nd wedding anniversary today but no big slap up meal is planned, it is just food that is easy to swallow and a day to celebrate being together. I am not ready or prepared to lose my soulmate to this bastard disease and he is determined that he is not going anywhere soon.

I have heard friends say oncology, oncologist and never really gave it a thought that one day we would rely on one to save my husbands life but here we are, at their mercy. I know we are very lucky that our hospital has such a great reputation and I am 100% sure that the oncologists are fantastic at what they do. It is still extremely surreal though that it is happening to us. (It is happening to us though isn't it? Are you sure it isn't a dream?)

I spend every waking hour feeling sad and shit scared about what is going to happen. I go to bed thinking what if and I wake up in the middle of the night feeling the same. It is emotionally draining and consuming but you just have to go with it because there is nothing we can do, it is all out of our control.

We had an impromptu meeting with a robotic surgeon which they squeezed in as ideally they wanted us to see him before the oncology meeting. The new plan of attack is … it has definitely not spread and it is a 5cm tumour between 23 and 28cm down his oesophagus. They are going for both chemotherapy and radiotherapy combined. The surgeon went all through the operation in great detail, including drawing us pictures and explaining what would be happening. Basically they take his stomach and make a new oesophagus out of the top part of it by pulling it up, cut the cancer out and join the two together. It will be 6-8 weeks after the treatment and will take 10 hours minimum. He said there are not many operations that are that long and he made a point of stating, make no mistake, this is major surgery but the mortality rate is 3% so you have a massive chance of beating this and it being successful. We are so lucky that our hospital have Da Vinci robots so the whole operation will be done robotically. This will make recovery time and scarring a lot better than if he had open surgery. He probably won't be able to ever eat big meals again, just little and often which is fine, neither of us care about that as long as he us alive at the end of it. He said the whole thing from start of treatment to full recovery will be roughly 9 months provided there are no complications but 40% of people have at least one blip along the way.

We cannot focus on that though, we will deal with each situation as and when it is needed. We are both happy that it is operable but it is still daunting to think that he will be having major life altering surgery. We have no option though and it was never in any doubt that we would ever question what the experts feel is best for Graham.

Just back from oncology. It went really well, we met with our dietician, cancer nurse and our consultant Dr Cummins. It was explained that it will be 4 and a half weeks of chemo once a week by drip and 5 days a week of radiotherapy. He said the last 2 weeks will be very challenging as the radiotherapy is increased each day and the last 2 weeks he will find it extremely challenging but it is doable with determination. Then it will be 4-6 weeks rest period to get over the treatment and get back to being healthy enough to be signed over to the surgeon for the big robotic op. He is making an appointment for a special CT scan that pinpoints the exact cancer position and then they mark him with 3 tattoo dots that show where the radiotherapy has to hit, there are lasers around the room so that he is in exactly the same position each day. He is also going to book in the start of treatment and will call us this week with dates. He was very reassuring and explained everything to us pausing for any questions we may have. After the big op 'if' he gets the all clear then no more treatment but if they think there is anything that has potential to crop up, he will go on immunotherapy for a year which is fine as there are not many bad side effects to that (we hope). It will be a monthly injection and is part of a current trial. He said we are going to get through this with you both and our goal is totally curative ! And do you know what? I believe him.

So now we know the exact plan of attack and that our whole team are rooting for us and doing everything they can to get rid of Grahams unwelcome visitor once and for all.

Today is Wednesday 28th June, we received a letter saying a kidney test has been booked for Thursday the 6th of July. It will be an Injection of radioactive dye at 10.30am, followed by a blood test at 12.30, 1.30 and 2.30pm. I panicked, this wasn't mentioned ...... what is the problem with his kidneys..... is this a setback? I called our GI nurse who said it is totally routine, it is just to see how the kidneys are functioning and how well they will do during chemo. Ok, a sigh of relief.

They don't necessarily tell you these things, they just book them in and if you have any questions it is down to you to ask which I actually agree with because there is so much to take in, it is easier to ask in your own time if you have any questions or concerns. The great thing is to know that we have someone at the end of the phone when anything comes up and no question is a silly one. They are so helpful and lovely and explain things in a language that we all understand and not in doctors jargon.

Next on the new job of being Grahams secretary, I received a call from the physio department, we need to book an appointment with you and Graham for Friday the 7th of July just to run through treatment diet, pre operation diet, exercises, side effects from chemo and radiotherapy and how they can be reduced and managed, support for us both and to talk through what shape he needs to be in for the big op.

I also remembered his cardiac and lung function test had been booked at 4pm on the 6th so the poor bugger will be at the hospital from 10.30am until probably 5pm that day so I need to prepare his nutrition drink and pack a lunch for him. There is a coffee shop and a M&S at our hospital but sandwiches and pastries are a big no no when your oesophagus is narrowed and eating isn't easy. It is things like this that you need to plan for as we cannot afford a day of not eating when every calorie counts in keeping his weight stable. It is like packing when you have a child. Drinks and snacks that are suitable because buying something when you are out and about is not an option at the minute.

My lessons so far …. Take a pen and note book to every appointment, do not panic if they call and ask can you come in tomorrow, cry and I mean really sob (honestly it helps), liaise with your work and keep them in the loop every step of the way, talk about cancer with your nearest and dearest if you can/want to, take each day at a time, plan meals and snacks and batch cook if you can and must not forget … must be strong for him.

Today we had another call from the radiotherapy department to book in the special tattoo CT scan on Monday. I said that is absolutely fine as he has got his kidney test on Thursday along with the cardio & lung test followed by the dietician, pre operation physiotherapy etc on Friday so nothing clashes date wise. I was then told that any test that uses contrast dye must be done at least 7 days apart and both the CT and kidney test use it. So we rescheduled (get used to rescheduling and juggling) It has now been rearranged that it is Monday for the CT,

Thursday for the cardio & lung test and Friday for the dietitian, physio, pre op appointment and the kidney test is now 10.15am, 12.15pm, 1.15pm and 2.15pm on the 12th of July. We were also told that the plan is for first chemo and radiotherapy to be started on July 26th. We are moving at a pace now and to be honest, it helps because you feel like the start of this battle is happening and you are not just waiting in limbo. Buy a calendar if you do not have one or do as I did and write it all on a magnetic white board so you can wipe it out and change as necessary.

Graham has had his first tattoo! He has got 3 tiny permanent tattoo dots either side of him and one in the middle so now he is all lined up to be in exactly the same position every day when he has his radiotherapy. It is funny as we can look at him now and see exactly where the tumour is which is weird. They kept putting him in the CT scanner bit by bit measuring it all out, then put in the contrast dye and did it again. He said it was slightly uncomfortable because he had his arms above his head holding onto a bar and had a box balancing on his stomach to measure how high and low his stomach went when he was taking deep breaths so it is all measured to the millimetre. Clever stuff that truly amazes me.

Another call today, we need a separate lung test as the radiotherapy will affect his lungs so they will be calling to book that in, they are trying to tie it in with either Thursdays fitness test or Fridays appointment. After all of these tests there will not be a part of his body that hasn't been seen or tested bless him. It is all for his safety though and there is a reason for each one. For someone who has never been into hospital before, he now needs a season ticket.

You will be amazed at what you can do with mince so I have recently learnt. The usual Cottage pie, chilli, mince and mashed potatoes, mince and onions but also mince with lentils & ras el hanout, spicy mince with cous cous, curried mince, mince with tiny chopped veg. I am getting good at trying to make slidey food tasty. Graham is lucky that he can still eat small cut easily digestible food at the minute, that may change once his radiotherapy starts as apparently it inflames the oesophagus and tumour but we will see. For the time being he is living on mince, mince, and more mince and very small diced chicken thighs in various sauces, protein porridge, shakes from the doctor and soft desserts. But I am not complaining as he is eating well and that is what counts. I find every single cancer a bastard but this one is awful because it is taking away one of life's fundamental functions that is eating. It doesn't help that Graham absolutely loved his food and we used to cook different things each week. I am not sure he will ever have a love for food again but there are a lot worse off so we need to count our blessings. I eat my meals separately from Graham because it isn't fair eating nice things in front of him. I also try to not have anything that is too smelly to tease him. We have separate items in the fridge now, low fat Mayo for me and full fat for Graham, semi skimmed milk for me and full fat for him and so it goes.

The cardio lung exercise test has just finished, they stopped it as he had completed it! They put a clip on his nose and a breathing tube in his mouth and he said he could have carried on but they said a big well done, you have done amazing. They are going to do a heart ultrasound just to be sure because of the left bundle branch block but they are very happy with him.

He had to ride on an exercise bike for about 10 minutes with them altering the resistance and for someone who doesn't cycle, he was surprised at how well he did but it proves he is fit and ready for what is going to be thrown at him. This was the one test that I wasn't concerned about but funnily enough, Graham was. He thought he may not of been fit enough but he proved himself wrong.

Today was the 1.30pm appointment at physiotherapy, Literally just got back at 3.30. Very lovely lady called Rachel who tested Grahams grip strength, made him do a walk test and then as many sit to standing and back down again on a chair in a minute so she has a base line of his current fitness. She said that he is extremely fit and has a great base for surgery. He has got home exercises to do which are all printed out and have been explained how many to do. What she said was that he is very fit but chemo and radio will knock him so it is her job to make sure he doesn't dip too much and then when he gets the 4-6 weeks rest before the op she will be working him harder to get to peak fitness again. There is a free gym there and they do online classes too which is amazing and shows again how lucky we are with our local hospital. She is also there for us to help if he gets bad side effects and cannot exercise as much so it will all be bespoke to him. She asked him how is his mental health and he said it's all good, he is just taking one hurdle at a time and she was the first person to ask at the hospital how I was coping, which made me burst into tears but once I had composed myself I said honestly I am fine too it was just nice to hear her being concerned about me. We had a brief chat about surgery and Rachel said that she will help us keep Graham at peak fitness if we need her.

Next stop on this rollercoaster is the 4 hour kidney test next Wednesday so a few days respite is on the cards. Graham is getting fed up of not being able to eat anything with texture and he is desperate for bbq lamb chops. It absolutely breaks my heart to say no but I am shitting myself that he may choke. Hardly first world problems I know but it is so very hard to not be able to eat what you want so he has promised me that he will take tiny bites and chew, chew, chew …… AND he actually ate them all!! It was lovely seeing his eyes light up while he was enjoying them so much bless him. It is silly things like that, that you take for granted. It is like taking a child into a sweet shop and saying I know it all looks lovely but you can't have any. Be thankful for every little triumph and today managing lamb chops was definitely a success.

It is now Monday the 10th July and we have had the call to book in for a heart ultrasound just to be extra sure that his heart will take the operation and to make sure there are no underlying issues which can be the case sometimes with left bundle branch block. So that has been booked in for this Friday. Another week of work/hospital balance which is fine as it is all for the greater good.
Change of plan, (really get used to this) they need to book in a different lung test ready for radiotherapy so the 4 hour kidney test is still tomorrow and the heart ultrasound followed by lung function test is now booked for Monday 17th. So a quick message to Grahams work to let them know that he will now be in for work on Friday but will need next Monday off instead. Grahams boss has been fantastic throughout this, supporting him all the way. He just wants a fit cancer free Graham back, however long it takes.

I think that is now all tests booked in prior to chemo radio but we are not holding our breath or taking anything for granted. Graham had a little issue swallowing today but we are not sure if we are clutching at straws and are not wanting to think about the possibility that the tumour is growing but we think it seems to be harder when he has been working all day and eating on the run because he is a delivery driver going to pubs and restaurants humping heavy crates of meat so not sure if that is playing a part or not. We will find out when he finishes work and treatment starts. This is the time when every little ache he gets, I think it has spread. It is on my mind 24/7 and the poor bugger can't even sneeze without me panicking. I need to get that under control as it isn't helping either of us.

I sent Graham off this morning for his 4 hour kidney test with his bottle of cordial, milky ways and a flask of soup. Luckily when the nurse asked him if he had refrained from caffeine he said yes but then she mentioned chocolate and he said I have some with me. So pleased that the nurse mentioned it because neither of us even thought about chocolate having caffeine in it so that could have scuppered the whole days testing ! He had his radioactive dye injected and then had the 3 blood tests over the next 4 hours so that is another test out of the way. Just the heart and lungs test to go. Tonight I am going to cook him some nice fresh salmon with new potatoes in butter which will be a change from mince and finely diced chicken. He is still in great spirits and really is taking this all in his stride so far. He said that once this is all over he wants a job at the hospital showing visitors where every department is as he will have been to most of them by the time this is over.

Today was the heart ultrasound and half hour pre radiotherapy lung test, I was feeling completely anxious that they would find underlying heart disease or something untoward that was causing his left bundle branch block. Here it comes, the stumbling block, not eligible for surgery, too high risk, sorry but we are going to pull the rug from under you and it is now palliative care. BUT the lady doing the ultrasound said everything looks healthy ! Wait, what! All that worrying and everything looks healthy! Great news. Apparently quite a few people have it with no underlying problems so they are happy. I really think after all this I will need therapy of some sort, it eats away at you and you are constantly on edge. Honestly the stress and worry really does take its toll. Next was the lung test, it ended up only being 20 minutes of sitting on a stool in what can only be described as a shower cubicle with a peg on his nose and a tube in his mouth, he had to go through various breathing in and out exercises and in the end they said it all looks very good. So we are good to go! Next stop is chemo radio to start shrinking this bastard once and for all.

I have been thinking of different meals for Graham as this progresses, I have currently got a chicken in the oven to make him a homemade soup with fresh turmeric, garlic and ginger and I am planning a beef soup that I will also blitz, Thai curry, fish pie and that sort of thing, anything to get away from mince for a little bit poor bugger. It honestly breaks your heart when the person who means the absolute world to you says I really fancy KFC, chips, steak, pork chop, toast and you say but you know you will not be able to swallow that and they say no I know with a look that is like telling a child that they cannot have any treats.

God this is a bastard disease and we have not even started treatment yet. I try telling myself that tears will not change anything and that what will be will be, but I truly know what cry me a river means now. Anyway, stop crying and get the ice cream maker out and make him some scrummy ice cream. Remember, must be strong for him.

It has been a good couple of days so far and we are both gearing up for treatment to start next week, in fact we are looking forward to it. It is Grahams birthday on Tuesday and instead of the usual slap up meal, it will just be easily swallowable food and instead of the usual clothes and bits, this year I have got him a silk pillowcase to help his hair and skin during chemo, some slippers for when he goes in for his op, a furry single sheet for if he needs to sleep on the recliner sofa, some fluffy socks in case he gets cold feet as I have been told that can be a side effect, some Bachs rescue remedy comfort & reassure and some hydration & electrolyte effervescent tablets and I wooden heart plaque saying 'be strong now because things will get better. It might be stormy now but it won't rain forever'. I never once thought I would be buying my husband a bloody care package to 'celebrate' his 62nd birthday but here we are. I am trying to have normal days and I actually found myself forgetting he has cancer a few times and for those moments it has been wonderful but then it taps me on the shoulder and says Don't forget about me, I am here to test you both physically and mentally so buckle up kids, it's going to be one hell of a journey. Human emotions are an odd thing, I wish I could just wake up and find that this whole thing was just a bad dream instead of feeling nervous, anxious, upset, concerned and shit scared every single bastard day.

It is strange what cancer or any serious illness can do to a relationship, I have always loved Graham with all my heart but I actually feel as though I love him more which sounds odd but I feel as though I need to protect him now and look after him and support him mentally but it is also so very hard not to feel sorry for him too. He doesn't want sympathy, he wants positivity and fun and that is not always easy. I watch him sadly working his way through his mushy meals and a bit more of my heart breaks each and every single day. I honestly do not want to think of the mental impact this will have on us at the end of our journey let alone the physical ones too for him. But remember, one day at a time. I have had my cry writing this paragraph and Graham is on his way back from work so I need to wash my face, get my shit together and greet him with a smile as always because remember…. Must be strong for him. It is like a little pickaxe that chips away at you each day leaving shattered fragments of who and what you used to be behind. Graham used to come in from work every day and ask what is for dinner but now he just comes in, has a shower and gets changed and just chats about his day. Food isn't exciting anymore.

We received a letter today that is a copy of what our oncologist has sent to our GP, it hit me like a tonne of bricks as we have never been told the staging or anything other than caught early, no spread but this letter says Squamous Cell Carcinoma T3 N2 M0. So now we know it is stage 3 and is in some lymph nodes but no spread, I feel totally overwhelmed and deflated. I have gone from looking forward to our future to thinking is this gruelling treatment and surgery going to be worth it and am I going to lose him. I posted on an oesophageal cancer Facebook group that I am a member of about what has happened.

I have had nothing but positive stories of people who were diagnosed the same and a lot worse than Graham and who have come through treatment and surgery and are all clear of cancer and living great lives. I feel much better about it now and I am looking at the positives, it has not spread, it is not stage 4, it is treatable, it is still curable, so let the journey begin and let us get Graham cancer free.

Drumroll please, Today was day one of kicking cancers arse ! We arrived ready for chemo and went in feeling good that treatment was starting.

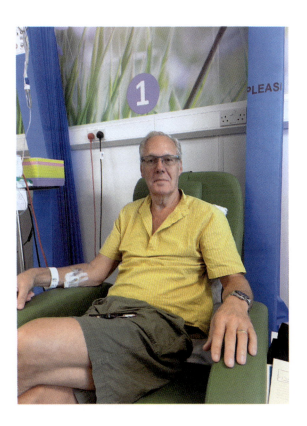

Graham sat down at the chemo chair and had his blood oxygen checked, temperature and blood pressure done. I looked at him and it hit me, I burst into tears and had this overwhelming feeling of sadness that I couldn't control so I kissed him and made a swift exit which of course upset him too. My plan was to be there the whole time but I failed miserably on that front. I took a walk, sobbed uncontrollably and then started to tell myself that today was a good day, today was round 1 of 5 chemo and round 1 of 23 radiotherapy, today was the start of this bastard shrinking ! Today was the day that we start taking back control of this thing growing inside of him. So I went back into the cancer centre, yes The Cancer Centre, just in case people don't know why they are there. Don't get me wrong, I get that it is a cancer centre but it is actually so very sad. I would like them all to be called Hope Centres or fighting centres or warriors centre, but it is a cruel world and cancer is cancer. Anyway, I went back in and my boy looked ok, they pulled a chair over for me to be with him for the rest of the treatment.

They only allow visitors for the first chemo because it can become too crowded, doesn't that tell you something about how many poor fuckers are fighting this bastard disease.

Graham had anti sickness medication, steroid, saline flush, first chemo, saline flush, second chemo and then finished off with a saline flush which took 4 and a half hours from start to finish as the first one is given slowly in case of allergic reactions which is totally understandable as people react differently. My boy was so brave and took it all in his stride, love him. He was perfectly fine sitting with his iPad reading the paper to while away the time.

They have a trolley that come around with teas and coffees and at lunchtime with soups, sandwiches, rolls and lots of treats that are all free which is amazing. Graham said soup please and when the lady said would you like a sandwich or bread roll with that, my heart broke again when he said unfortunately I can't eat any bread but thank you anyway. Fuck, I really hate this with every fibre of my being. We then went downstairs for radiotherapy which was a 10 minute blast. So that is day one finished. We have got 3 different meds that are taken at various times so I have had to make notes for each day so we know what's what. We were also told that it will be blood tests every Monday just to make sure all is ok with the chemo and to nip any problems in the bud.

It was a long day and we both felt drained but confident now treatment had started so fingers crossed his little visitor will now stop growing and start withering and dying.

A great nights sleep was had and Graham woke feeling well and rested, he has got to take 1 tablet 3 times and 1 tablet twice today, and a final one that is just for a couple of days. These are to help with side effects so it is vital they are taken on time. His appetite is still good so it will be porridge for breakfast, mid morning nutrition shake, soup for lunch and then sweet & sour finely diced chicken thighs later with a jacket potato followed by some frozen yoghurt and double cream to keep those calories up. As he has stopped working while treatment is ongoing, his exercises start today so after this mornings radiotherapy, he is going for a walk and do some strength exercises that the physiotherapist gave him. He is determined to keep as fit as possible.

I printed a countdown sheet and put it on the fridge so each day Graham can strike off that day and see that the end in sight. It's funny as now I feel as though we are in control now.

Now Grahams immune system is taking a battering it is time to shield him to try our best at avoiding any infections so no shellfish, blue or soft cheese, rare meat and no visiting from anyone who has even the slightest sniffle. I know we can't wrap him up in cotton wool but we have to try our best and be sensible. As chemo is evident in bodily fluids, the toilet seat is disinfected after every use, towels & bedding washed regularly, hands washed every opportunity, no rolling over onto his side of the bed and keeping everything as clean as it can be. We have to check his temperature daily and go straight to a&e if it drops too low or raises too high and show Grahams cancer card, yes there really is a cancer card! People may joke about having one to get out of doing things but they really do exist. It bypasses the a&e queue and gets you seen straight away because certain infections can be extremely serious to someone with a weakened immune system and time is of the essence in getting treatment. I was desperate to get him sitting outside in the fresh air as much as possible but in true British summer style, it's due to rain for the next week at least.

We have had a lovely weekend, Graham is not suffering from any side effects yet so it was nice to be normal for a couple of days other than the medication regime in his Cycle 1 chemotherapy bag. In between the rain we even managed to sit outside for a few hours soaking up some vitamin D and getting some fresh air which always makes things feel better.

I am not looking forward to next week as I think it will be when the radiotherapy really kicks in and irritates his skin, makes him tired and feeling crappy but we will see. I wouldn't be surprised if he takes it all in his stride to be honest. I have seen lots of stories about people who can eat normally after 2 rounds of chemo and a week of radio but it seems to be 50/50 as to whether it gets a whole lot easier to eat or whether it gets inflamed making it even harder. I am not religious at all but I am praying that it gets easier for him and he can have food that he is really missing which will also help keep his weight up and more importantly keep his spirits up too.

Today was blood tests and 4th radiotherapy followed by a telephone appointment to see how he was doing. They asked him if he had felt sick, been sick, had any pins and needles in his hands and feet, loss of appetite, trouble sleeping, swallowing getting worse or any other concerns to which he said no, none of those so they are very happy with his progress so far. He has been suffering with constipation for a few days which apparently is very common with one of his anti sickness meds so he has been taking stool softener that we got from the local chemist which doesn't seem to be working. He was in so much discomfort yesterday that he actually said this is so uncomfortable, I'm not sure it is all worth it. He didn't mean it but I thought bloody hell, if he is thinking of throwing in the towel just because he can't have a poo, he really will not be able to cope when the going gets really tough. It really upset me but I don't think I realised quite how much discomfort he was in and how much it was getting him down. You are given a phone number to call at any time during treatment in case you have any concerns or problems or just general questions.

I called the helpline or chemo hotline as it is called and they said they will prescribe him some more medication to take daily when he goes in for chemo this week which should ease the constipation but in the meantime to go and get him some suppositories. Graham walked to our local pharmacy with me to keep up his steps and we came back with what we needed. Without going into detail, suppository in and 20 minutes later we had progress! He had a sore tummy and felt rough still but at least we now had movement. Within an hour he had been a couple of times more and the old Graham was back, feeling back to normal and being his old determined and happy self. I was really surprised at quite how shit (excuse the pun) he had felt.

One thing to check and double check is appointments across different departments. The Chemo appointment card has his chemo, blood tests with times and telephone appointments on it and we were told that we needed to book the bloods online which is fine. His radiotherapy sheet had radio and blood appointments on it saying they were already booked so I called radio and they said yes the bloods are already booked in but when Graham arrived, it hadn't been booked at all and he was told that we need to book them online. It is no problem but it is worth checking and double checking when you have daily appointments across departments. It was no problem and the blood department were great and squeezed him in as soon as he explained what had happened. After a few calls backwards and forwards with our nurses, it seems that the chemo card is incorrect as the telephone appointments should be face to face because you have to see a consultant weekly when you are on radiotherapy and the radiotherapy sheet was incorrect saying bloods had been booked.

Confused? You will be. But it is all now resolved that Mondays will be radio followed by blood test followed by seeing the consultant in the clinic. I booked the blood tests in online so we are back on track and know what we are doing each day.

We haven't had any calls about his blood test so we are to presume no news is good news so it is back today for radiotherapy blast number 5, some exercises later along with some walking and getting some fresh air. Drinking lots of water is also important when you are having treatment so we fill a big bottle up each morning so we know how much he has drunk throughout the day. I have to be cautious who I mix with too because the last thing I want to do is bring home an infection or a cold so I feel like I am shielding as well. It is like the pandemic all over again.

Sadly It didn't go to plan this afternoon, Graham was fine after radiotherapy but he has got some phlegm that feels like it is stuck so he is going to have a check with the nurses tomorrow when he goes for chemo. He went to bed at 4pm not feeling very well so it is starting to look like he may not be great with the treatment after all, he is not himself and is very snappy and miserable. He has lost a few pounds this week too because he is not eating properly. But to be fair, 5 days of constipation and feeling really uncomfortable is the reason for that but now we are back on track with food so that should improve. I truly believed he was giving up which was heartbreaking as he was so determined from day one but I am sure now that it was just a blip and I guess it is to be expected to have crappy days. Constipation is not to be taken lightly, it was awful for him.

My happy place used to be in the kitchen, I used to post regularly on social media with my cooking. I loved it, I loved trying new things, I loved coming up with recipes, I loved cooking celebrity chefs recipes, but now my kitchen is a place for soft food, diced food, sloppy food. It is like my comfort blanket has been ripped away from me. If ever I felt down I used to bake something, if ever we had anything to celebrate I used to create meals but that has now all gone. Graham used to watch cookery shows and ask can you make that next week but now he watches them and just says that looks lovely, I will be able to eat that when this is all over. It is great that he is looking to the future and he has no doubt that he will be tucking into scrummy food at some point.

Ok today is another day, we are both a lot more positive today and back on track. I called our nurse and she said that it is not phlegm, it is food sticking higher up and is totally normal as it is caused by inflammation from radiotherapy which may get better or may not as treatment goes on but for now he has been advised to have a sloppier diet with 3 nutritional shakes a day instead of 2 so we know that it is 'normal' which is a HUGE relief! Honestly you get used to thinking that any little ache or feeling is cancer related, it is natural I guess to feel that way at the minute. Natural to feel that way!? There is nothing natural about this, it's a nightmare but you know where I am coming from.

Graham got a call to arrive 2 hours later than normal for his chemo as there had been a problem with it being delivered. He turned up as requested and was directed to the appropriate room.

So far he has been sitting in a corridor for nearly 2 hours none the wiser to when or if it is arriving today. He has to have his radiotherapy within an hour after chemo and that is booked for 1.54pm and it is now 1pm so that is not going to happen today. Hoping they will still squeeze him in if or when he gets his chemo done. It is nobody's fault, these things happen and Graham is so patient. Problems happen and you just have to go with it, please don't kick off to the staff. They are doing their best and trying to help you so don't treat them like shit.

He was sent to radiotherapy for his 1.54pm appointment and then back to chemo, they had his second chemo bag but were still waiting on his first one which eventually came and he was hooked up at 4pm. Apparently the hour in between is not critical as they still work together. Not sure how long it will take as it should be normal speed today because it is his second one so no need to do the slow release this time in case of any reactions.

He is going to be so tired by the time he gets home and unwind but hopefully I can get some food down him before he crashes. 2 chemo down, 3 to go, 6 radiotherapy down, 17 to go. Graham was in good spirits when he got home at 6.20pm considering how long a day he had, he had some soup and a nutritional shake, watched some tv and went to bed for some needed rest.

Today is a great day, Graham got up at 7.30am and said I feel great, I am going out for a walk. He came back and had a big bowl of full fat yoghurt and a nutrition drink. Then he went off T o radio, came home and had homemade soup, a shake and a cup of tea followed by 2 milky ways and a bag of Wotsits so it is all good. We are both in a good place about what is going on and for today, I am hugely grateful.

Life can be like an up and down, twisting rollercoaster at times but you just have to roll with it and deal with it as best as you can. The positive feelings we both have are that treatment is working and his hidden visitor is shrinking. We have to believe that.

We had an ok weekend, Graham is finding it hurts when he swallows which we are assuming is radiation inflammation. Because of this he is not eating properly which is totally understandable so his weight will drop again and he will start losing strength too. We are going to see the consultant this morning so hopefully they can help because at this rate we could get into trouble. He is not really keeping up with walking because he feels so shit but he is doing his weights and exercises which is great considering how he is feeling. I am not moaning anymore as understandably he just snaps at me and tells me to leave him alone so I have decided that as hard as it is to watch him like this, it is his decision and his life and not mine. The same goes for eating, I just get snapped at and he knows he is not eating enough so I am not saying a word as I really don't want him to feel any worse than he already does. He cannot help it bless him, it is just so frustrating for him poor bugger. I honestly didn't think it would be this crappy after only a week and a half of treatment, they said the last 2 weeks will be extremely challenging, well let me tell you, this isn't a walk in the park so far. We know it has to be done and we know it is for the best but it's still bloody hard.
I actually ate a full meal for the first time in ages which made me feel a bit better but to be honest, I thought I was emotionally strong but it is so hard being shouted at one minute, apologised to the next, utter contempt to praise in the blink of an eye.

Don't get me wrong, I love him with all my heart and I know he loves me too, he is going through an awful lot and it truly is not his fault. He is still a bloody trooper and we both just find this bastard disease hard to deal with. We will get through this together but I want people who are sadly in our situation to know that it is normal to have really shitty days. People will say 'it's ok it is curable', 'you are one of the lucky ones as they said it is a curative path', 'you are going to be ok', 'it will soon all be over'…. You will want to smash their heads against a brick wall and scream at them and say but it is a living nightmare and he may not be ok he may not survive this, our lives will never be the same again, his body will never be the same again. Oh but don't worry, it's curable! People mean well and I know that but it is funny how you start thinking about things. Someone may say the queue at Sainsbury's was a nightmare which is a perfectly normal thing to say but you find yourself thinking it's just a bloody queue, my husband has cancer and I don't know if I will lose him. It is not fair and you know it isn't fair but you still feel like it at times. Life goes on and you have to remember that, we all have worries and problems.

I am trying to be positive today, it is radiotherapy number 9 followed by his blood test and then onto the consultants clinic so we will see what they say.
Just got back from our meeting and Graham explained how eating was painful because of the inflammation from his radiotherapy sessions. She straight away has given him liquid medication to take 30 minutes before eating and also 1000mg of effervescent paracetamol 4 times a day to help. She was dead chuffed that he is getting no nausea or pins & needles or cold sensitivity from chemo and said it is all going to plan so far.

She did also explain that the pain will probably get worse as he still has 14 radio to go but there is plenty of scope to up his liquid medication if/when needed. She also said to look forward to being able to eat what he wants within 2 weeks of treatment finishing, ready to build him up for his robo op. We briefly discussed a feeding tube and the whole team are in agreement with us that it is to be avoided unless absolutely necessary and let us try the medication route first. The good thing is that the oncologist wasn't surprised at all that Graham was in pain, she made a point of saying it is perfectly normal but they rely on you telling them if you struggle as everyone is different. We went straight to the hospital pharmacy and picked up his new medication so it can be started straight away.

Graham managed some soft roasted potatoes with gravy, a big portion of creme caramel with clotted cream, 2 nutrition shakes and a bag of Wotsits, so not a lot for an entire day but I cannot seem to get him to eat 3 meals a day plus his shakes but as I said before, I am not moaning at him anymore. He went to bed at 5.30pm because he was so tired which is fine and totally normal but I think maybe he is getting bored doing nothing and in turn, doing nothing makes you tired. It could well be radiotherapy or/and chemo lethargy or it maybe not walking enough although the physio did say that there will definitely be days where he won't exercise, it really could be his body saying ok I am in need of rest now. It is so hard to know but i am not saying anything as he is a grown man and if I am honest, I think he is still getting his head around all of this which is totally understandable as the poor bastard cannot eat properly, cannot work, knows his life has changed forever so who am I to deny him a few lazy days.

The one thing I do find is that it is so hard to watch your loved one like this, we try to coax them not really understanding how they feel. Graham is a very strong man and if he is struggling I dread to think what some of you are going through. There are also very sweet but sad times when Graham eats something and asks did I do well? He knows I am trying and I know he is trying too. He looked at me and said I need to build myself up and be your big strong boy again. God I love him so much.

Today was another shit day, graham had his 10th radio but he only got up half an hour before he was due to go as his chest was hurting. He came home and sat on the sofa all day and went to bed at 2.30pm, getting up at 5pm saying his chest hurt again so he sat on the sofa and said I am going back to bed I don't want food. So after putting it back in the fridge, he then said actually I will give it a go as I need to eat so he had his liquid meds, waited for it to work and attempted a finely chopped butter chicken dish and he ate all of it! followed by some cold creme caramel and a big dollop of clotted cream so the day has ended well. We also had an honest conversation with each other that I am pissing him off by not understanding how he feels and he is pissing me off by not getting motivated while he can, so we have agreed that we both know where the other one is coming from and it helped for us both to air our frustrations and we now have a joint agreement about how we go forward.

We have had a good few days, no chest pain and swallowing not as painful as it has been so the medication is clearly working. We will see how the weekend goes as to whether he needs them altering or changing at the next consultant meeting on Monday.

He has just done his exercises in the garden and even ate some Brie with Ritz crackers which is a bit of a triumph. So far today he has eaten protein porridge, 2 nutrition shakes, a bag of Wotsits, oxtail soup and his cheese & crackers. Tonight he is going to try a minced and moist fish pie that we got from an online company who do a range of meals for people with dysphagia. Neither of us like the idea of ready meals but we are giving them a go as they will come in handy after surgery as they do a puréed range too which will help me save some time when I am caring for him during his rehabilitation. They are nutritionally balanced and at least he will be getting tasty flavours each day. I am happy if he has breakfast, lunch, some snacks and then his oven meal in the evening.

I think it has finally sunk in with both of us that this journey is now underway and changes have had to be made both physically and mentally. Be prepared to tighten your belts as cancer is expensive. Different foods, loss of work, hobbies or books to pass the time, travelling to and from appointments etc etc. Everyones financial situation is different and I would advise speaking to the citizens advice about what you are or are not entitled to as every little helps. We were not entitled to anything but lots of people are. Anyway enough of money talk, we are over half way and the end is in sight, 10 radio and 2 chemo to go! We are off for a walk this morning and making the most of Grahams weekend off of treatment, let's hope the weather is kind. It is funny how life is now Monday to Friday treatment and the weekend is our time.

Since the 10th of May we have learnt that Cancer is a bastard disease that can pick absolutely anyone to attack and treatment can be hard both mentally and physically.

Relationships need a bit of extra work as it is very easy to become the carer and nagger instead of husband and wife, money is tighter, boredom from not working kicks in so you need things to keep you occupied, exercise is really important for recovery and mental health, you really find out who your true friends are. But most importantly we have learnt that we are still a strong couple, we still love each other and Graham will ring that bloody bell with all his heart WHEN he is cancer free.

Well what a fantastic day we have had. We went to the hospital this morning and Graham had his radiotherapy followed by his blood test and then we went in to see the consultant. Graham explained that his one and only issue is the pain he gets when eating, he described it as swallowing razor blades. The consultant said ok don't worry, we will get your pain under control so let us stop the 1000mg of paracetamol and replace it with Co Codamol along with oxetacaine and see how that goes but if he still struggles then he must not wait until next weeks appointment, he is to tell radiotherapy and they will arrange an alternative. We came home, he took his effervescent co codamol, followed by the oxetacaine liquid and waited half an hour or so for the liquid to work on his inflammation and …….. he ate 2 warmed croissant's with butter and homemade strawberry jam! He hasn't been able to eat bread in 3 months so this made us both so happy. The look on Grahams face was priceless, I didn't know whether to burst into tears or laugh with happiness. He said oh my god that was so nice, he actually enjoyed eating ! So if you find yourself in discomfort or any pain, talk to your team as they are prepared for all situations and they really will do their best until they have succeeded in keeping you comfortable.

The dysphagia meals will now stay in the freezer until post op which will be when he really needs them.

8 radio to go and 2 chemo! He is in no pain at all and is even asking for chips tonight. I am so chuffed at how he is doing. The consultant did say it will get worse but at the minute we are taking what we can get. He is so much happier now he can eat what he wants again and I can't say I blame him. Hoping for a KFC soon which will really lift his mood. Isn't it funny what you crave, I make homemade food all the time but we are both a sucker for fried chicken every now and again.

The good fortune has continued, radio and chemo today and he came home starving so had his nutrition drink and some Ritz crackers with homemade mackerel pate and this evening I barbecued him some lamb chops with fried cubed potatoes which is what he fancied and all went down a treat with no blockages and NO PAIN. I truly am so happy that eating is back on track, we know that the last week may be hard but I am getting the calories in him while I can. His mood is lifted and the sun is shining so we are both so happy and positive and taking the fact that he can swallow easier now as a sign that his tumour is shrinking/has shrunk. Remember it doesn't always go exactly as the specialists tell you, everyone is different. Some people are on morphine after this amount of radiotherapy so you must speak out if you are in pain.

Graham got sent his 2 yearly bowel screening test to do which he did and now we have received a letter saying that a telephone consultation is needed along with a colonoscopy leaflet. Honestly it doesn't rain, it bloody pours. I am praying that it is nothing sinister as neither of us can deal with anything else.

Grahams appetite has also gone down a bit too now from the chemo we are guessing as they did say it could happen which is such a shame as his swallowing is so much better. I am in a catch 22 because if I try to coax him to eat, he just shouts or storms off to bed telling me to leave him alone but if I don't say anything then I am just watching him lose weight. I cannot win this one so for the sake of my sanity I guess I will just have to watch him lose even more weight which is heartbreaking and needless but I totally understand that if he isn't hungry then he doesn't want to eat. It is so hard for him, he knows that he needs to eat, but his body is saying no way. Hoping it is a just a reaction to chemo and not because treatment isn't working and the cancer has spread to him stomach. See how quickly you can go from treatment must be working to oh no it's spread?

We went to see the consultant today and she is so pleased with how he is coping with treatment that she said I will change the next appointments to telephone calls ! She did say that as soon as treatment finishes it will be a big push to get his fitness back up and his weight. We spoke about the bowel screening test and she said she would expect it to come back positive as it will show the cancer that they know about, she also said to tell them that he is not having a colonoscopy until after the operation. But it is nothing to worry about at all. 4 radio and 1 chemo is all he has left which is amazing but I think the next big struggle will be getting his fitness back up to pre treatment levels, it is so hard for him as he is not working so is no longer doing physical work daily but I am praying the operation wont be delayed as he is showing signs of definitely not being anywhere near how he was pre treatment.

I guess this was to be expected but the hospital are happy so that is the main thing. On a good note though he did eat a sandwich and some porridge today so far but let us see what he manages this evening. He has totally gone off the nutrition shakes which I understand but he will now be losing hundreds of calories a day and not eating more to replace them but as long as he is eating 3 meals a day plus snacks we will be ok.

It's now 5.25pm and graham has gone to bed feeling dizzy from the co codamol which the consultant did say could be a side effect that will get better although he has been on them for a week so far, but he has not been out of bed long as he had a nap earlier so it is day 4 of no evening meal again, he did manage a third of a shake before he went to bed but as one shake is the equivalent to a sandwich according to our dietician, it is not much. But not much is better than nothing. He has done a little walking today to our friends house and back and walking around the hospital so that's something bless him.

It is honestly a bastard disease for anyone to cope with and Graham is one of the lucky ones in as much as little side effects but I do think it is taking it's toll now mentally and physically on both of us. Sometimes I no longer feel like his wife as we don't seem to have any couples moments at all anymore. It is just talk of tablets, eating, cancer and treatment. It is my job to care for him which is absolutely fine as I am happy to do it because I love him. This is not a poor me comment, I merely want you to know that it is normal. It is not all the time and it will pass.

We had the telephone consultation from the bowel screening and the lady explained that they do not have any medical records to look at, they only see the bowel screening results and nothing else.

As soon as we said about the diagnosed oesophageal cancer, she said that would explain the positive result and she also said that because Graham has had a pet scan, that would of shown up any nasties so we said about sending Graham another poo test kit after the op but apparently the computer only allows one test to be sent every 2 years so to get around it, we had to opt out of the screening programme and then after the op, we call them and opt back in which will allow a test to be sent out. So that is one thing dealt with until the end of the year.
I am praying that at some point I will see a glimpse of the old Graham but I am not convinced he will ever be back. Anyway tomorrow is another day and it is radiotherapy number 20 so let us see what the day brings.

We have had an ok couple of days.
Graham is very tired now which is to be expected, he was in bed most of the day yesterday and only getting up to eat but he did manage one shake and a kebab as that is what he fancied. I am really not sure when or if he will actually manage 3 meals a day. But I am not going to get hung up on food because if you feel sick, dizzy or tired it is the last thing you want. Realistically we knew there would be days of extreme lethargy but it isn't easy seeing such an active man so shattered. He must need it though because as soon as his head hits the pillow he sleeps. He is finding it so frustrating too, he is fed up of feeling shattered.

It is Grahams last chemo today, hoorah ! He started the day feeling very lightheaded and it really took a lot for him to go for his chemo and radio, he stood by the door with the frame holding him up but he soldiered on with all his might. I looked at him and thought there is no way he is going to make it today but he did.

He usually gets home at lunchtime so I am hoping he will be feeling a bit better and possibly hungry enough for some lunch later.

Graham felt somewhat better when he got home, he had his nutrition drink, a bag of Wotsits and a cup of soup at the hospital, he didn't go to bed for a snooze either. He then ate a Greek style meze that I had made and we both think that the help yourself style way of eating may suit him better as he is not looking at a whole plate of food and feeling pressurised into eating it.

I was standing at the worktop and Graham walked up to me and kissed me, I asked him what it was for and he said 'because I love you'. The other day I wondered if I would ever see the old Graham again and in that moment, he was back. It was perfect timing and it really meant so much.

I have had a read back over a few pages and I think I need to say that this really is not a poor me story, I merely hope to help people that are going through this that your feelings are normal and that I too have been there. I hope it may help if you feel guilty at feeling bad or just feel plain shit. It is not all fairies and rainbows, sometimes it is shitstorms and anger.

Stick with it, stick with your partner.

One day at a time. Let the anger be anger but not towards them, let the love be love 100% towards them. Talk to friends, cry, scream, feel lost but do not forget that you matter too, you need to eat, sleep and care for yourself. It is not always easy, in fact sometimes you just cannot find the strength or energy but they need us and they need us strong and capable.

Graham felt a lot better today and went off for his radiotherapy and came back ready for breakfast so he ate a nice bowl of protein porridge with some fresh fruit added. He feels as though he was really blasted today but he went and had a snooze and then got up and ate some beef strips in a veggie and tomato sauce to help him get some fibre. He is really trying to eat more and hopefully as the days go on it will improve once all the poison is out of his body.

It is the END OF TREATMENT DAY. Friday the 25th of August.
My boy has completed 23 radiotherapy and 5 chemo in 4 and a half weeks and I am so proud of him.
He is really suffering though today, his oesophagus is very sore so he has only managed a pancake with a small spoon of ice cream and one nutritional drink before going to bed. I am truly hoping that the poor bastard starts feeling better soon, I really feel for him. They said the soreness and feeling like crap could last up to 2 weeks but could also get better within a week so fingers crossed he is lucky.

Graham slept like a log and woke up feeling slightly better. He ate two boiled eggs with soldiers and a nutrition drink which is great, he went for a snooze at lunchtime to sleep off the crappy feeling for a bit but then got up ready for some dinner. I know that ideally we need him on 3 meals a day but if that is all he can manage, it is certainly better than nothing and can only improve as the days continue. We went for a walk round to the local pharmacy to pick up his meds and get some fresh air which was great. I am looking forward to being on the up each day fingers crossed.

We had a good day starting with graham eating breakfast and lunch and a nutrition drink. He was doing really well. He then went for a snooze but when it was time for his meds after being in bed for a couple of hours, he just said whatever. I reminded him again that he was an hour late for his meds but again I got a whatever so I am not forcing him, he is feeling so frustrated that he knows he is doing so well but keeps getting lightheaded. I did a bit of research and we are pretty confident that it is the co codamol that is making him feel dizzy and lightheaded which to be fair, Graham did say a few days ago that he was convinced it was them so we are onto plan b. Ditch the co codamol and go back to 1000mg of paracetamol because food is going down perfectly and as long as he isn't in any pain and the paracetamol controls it, we may be onto a winner. He had porridge for breakfast, cold meats and cheese biscuits for lunch and a very small plate of cauliflower cheese, gratin potatoes and chicken thighs in a creamy tomato sauce for dinner which is amazing considering how dizzy he felt, he did go to bed straight after dinner but that is fine. He needs his rest too as rest is recovery.

We haven't announced Grahams illness on Facebook or any social media and we haven't told very many people at all, not because we don't want people to know. It is more that it is our battle and when the time is right for us to tell the world, we will. Neither of us wanted lots of messages of I am so sorry or if there is anything I can do. Yes there is something you can do, take this bastard disease away from the love of my life.
We have of course told family and a handful of friends and the oesophageal cancer group on Facebook which really helps as I know we are not alone in this fight.

But there is no right or wrong, tell people if it helps but don't if that helps too. We are relatively insular in as far as socialising so for us it is like a regroup and fight this our way, we find strength in each other and that is what makes us a great team.

It is an odd time now because treatment is done and now it is a waiting game for the scan to find out if chemo radio has done its job so surgery can go ahead. It takes us back to the beginning of praying for positive results. We know the scan cannot be for at least 2 weeks after the last radio as they need all the radiation out of his body so it is time now to lead an as normal life as we can for a bit. Graham has purchased an exercise bike with resistance bands on it to start getting his strength and stamina back as he really will need it after robocop does its job on him. It seems surreal to think that we are getting him in tip top condition ready to be absolutely battered and in ICU having to start all over again but it is all for the greater good to get this disease killed once and for all. We will cross the bridge of feeding tubes, possible complications and long recovery one day at a time.

It has been an ok week after treatment, the dizziness in under control and the feeling really rough, in fact for the last 3 days Graham hasn't had an afternoon nap which is great but the pain when eating is back so now we are back to square one with him not wanting to eat. He has only had 1 day of eating 3 meals in months now but I totally understand that if it hurts, you do not want to do it so we have given in and gone back to co codamol to see if it helps him eat again and to see if the dizziness comes back. I know he has bad pain when he eats but he goes from the bed to the sofa and back again, he doesn't want me here.

I am an inconvenience that is just useful for fetching him drinks. There is no talking, he just stares at his iPad or the tv and answers me if he has too, usually followed by a sigh, it is easier for me to stay out of his way, I stay up in the kitchen or out in the garden if the weather is good. He used to love being out in the sun but I am lucky if he comes to sit in the garden for an hour and then it is usually about 4 as he goes to bed at 5 because he is usually shattered by then poor bugger. He is doing 20 minutes a day on his bike to start building up his fitness which is a big move in the right direction so credit where credit is due but we both know he will possibly end up with the operation being delayed if this carries on much longer but he said that's fine and he doesn't have a problem with it being delayed which sounds like he isn't bothered. Don't get me wrong, I know he doesn't mean it, he is annoyed and frustrated at feeling so crap and unwell but we both know that he will not get better if he doesn't eat but that is so hard when it hurts him to eat. If I said to you, here is your all time favourite meal but it will feel like swallowing razor blades when you eat every mouthful, would you eat it? Probably not is my guess. I am also slightly concerned that he isn't ever hungry anymore so even when the inflammation goes down and the pain goes, I am not sure he will even eat then but maybe he will and it is just the thought of it being painful that makes you feel not hungry. It is heartbreaking seeing him like this and the grumpy attitude is not like him at all, he is usually the jokey sarcastic one of us but cancer robs you of who you are. It chips away at you until you are broken.

Anyway, technically Graham should in theory wake up not in pain as he has been back on the co codamol since yesterday so we may have happy Graham back.

If it has gone to plan but let us see what todays roll of the dice will bring. Well today has started amazing! Graham has just eaten a chipolata, 2 eggs, half a buttered roll, one rasher of bacon, a slice of black pudding and some beans so we are getting back on track. I am so proud of him. Today is going to be a good day. He is looking good and feeling good so hopefully now it is onwards and upwards, we are having a heatwave this week so lots of sitting out and getting some vitamin d and fresh air is on the cards for both of us. Cherish the good days and enjoy them.

I have written down the dark days because you will have them and trust me, they are not pleasant. He is frustrated, I am frustrated, he is angry, I am angry and so it goes but never lose sight of the fact that sometimes it is cancer, chemo, radio and pain talking and not your loved one. It does get better and you really will get used to biting your tongue and crying but it is better than lashing out at them when they are already feeling rock bottom. Graham is upset that he isn't providing for me, he is upset that he cannot work, he is frustrated with feeling like shit and he is tired from all the tests and treatments. I looked back on some of this and thought about deleting some of the dark times but decided against it because they are real and they make you feel absolutely helpless but then you have a few good days and the bad ones become a distant memory. Graham hasn't read this yet but hopefully it will help him too by seeing it from my perspective although I bet he says I wasn't that bad or take that paragraph out but I won't because I want anyone reading this to not feel like it is only happening to them. We are a select group of this bastard disease. Some on the facebook group I belong to have lost their battle, some are on palliative care with hope of a longer life and some have had the all clear.

Some are living a great life years after the op. It is all down to what fate has in store. That roll of the dice. I spoke to a lady this morning who has a similar diagnosis to Graham but is now on palliative care because they couldn't remove all of the affected lymph nodes during surgery because they were too close to other organs. She is now fighting with immunotherapy to prolong her life. Imagine that, going through chemo and then getting strong enough for the major operation, recovering from that only to be told that they couldn't get it all out! Life is truly not fair, who deserves to get this disease? Who deserves to go through treatment hell to be told that it hasn't worked? Who deserves to get the all clear only to be told it is back? I am not a religious person but if I was I would be really questioning gods existence right now. No higher being would put great people through this. Imagine having young children, no partner or support group and going through this. Every single person battling cancer truly are warriors, they really are.

We have now found out that the dizziness and feeling awful is 100% co codamol, the pain has gone to be replaced by nausea, constipation and dizziness so he has decided that it is just not worth the side effects and as he is now 9 days post treatment so technically the inflammation should start easing soon, it is back to paracetamol. After 2 days, he is feeling great again and not in anywhere near as much pain as he was and no dizziness or feeling rough. We had to do a suppository again so he is back to being himself. It is different for everyone but if something is making you feel rough and you are not sure if it is the effects of treatment or the medication, double check with your team.

You know your own body so if it doesn't feel right, voice your concerns. It is you body, your battle and your instinct.

We received a letter for Grahams CT scan which will be on my birthday the 22nd of September, not that we were going out celebrating or anything. In fact I hope it is a good omen. The results will then go to the weekly oncologists meeting on Tuesday 26th September so any day after that, we will find out if the treatment has been successful and when the op is scheduled for. Fingers and toes crossed.

We are back on track now with eating fruit and 2, sometimes 3 meals a day with snacks and the nutrition drinks, exercises daily along with the bike riding and generally in a much better place physically and mentally, it was only a few days ago when I thought he was giving up but it now proves to me what pain and feeling unwell can really do to a person.

I have just read this from the beginning again and it seems like a lifetime ago, cancer is our new normal. Careful meal planning is our new normal. Trying to boost calories is our new normal but what is not normal anymore is pain control, worrying constantly, low moods and constant tiredness. It has only been 4 months and what a rollercoaster it has been. From utter despair, crying, bickering, low moods to positivity, energy and fighting spirit. He will come through the op not as one of the 40% who have complications but one of the 60% who doesn't, he will rehabilitate steadily and he will ring that bell when his unwelcome visitor is gone from our lives. Most people think an unwelcome visitor in a marriage is an affair, ours is a tumour.

Getting in between us, trying to take our feelings away and hacking away at our emotions and relationship. Well you haven't succeeded you bastard, in fact you have made us stronger so the joke is on you.

Graham is now hungry at meal times and although not eating huge amounts, he is eating. Instead of a burger and chips it's now 3/4 of a burger, instead of a plateful of food it's now a third of a plateful but it is huge progress and my boy is back. He is the usual annoying, sarcastic and funny person he always was. I have a new found admiration for him now too, he is a bloody warrior, he is a fighter, he is a legend and he is not giving up anytime soon.

We have started a list of things for his hospital bag and one thing I did buy was a luggage strap with his NHS number and surname on which I thought will come in handy if he is moved when in hospital so his belongings go with him. Chargers so he can communicate with the outside world, a kindle loaded with books to help the time go, along with the usual toiletries and clothing.

Our hospital has an open day on the 23rd of September and part of it is showing the Da Vinci robot. We cannot wait to go and see it in action and actually see it in the flesh so to speak. It will be a great opportunity to help get our head around what is going to happen when D day comes, in the meantime we are taking each day at a time and his eating is increasing each day, strength is increasing each day, generally being together is increasing each day. Today has been a great day, lots of sun, food, hydrating and exercises. I appreciate not everyone will go through exactly what we have, some have better staging of cancer and some will have worse.

Some may need a feeding tube and some may not, some may have nightmare side effects and some may not. This is merely our journey, it has had its ups and downs and it's tears and laughter but bugger me it really is a test. We have been through so much already but I guess realistically we are about to finish one hurdle and start another massive expedition with the operation.

We have been told that the op is 10 hours minimum so that will be a very very long worrying stressful day which I am not looking forward to at all but it has to be done. Grahams life will be in the hands of an extremely talented team who I know will do all they can for him. Graham is extremely confident about the operation and is actually excited by the thought of it being robotic.

The weather has been fantastic for September so far and we have spent lots of time in the garden, considering treatment only finished only 16 days ago, Graham is coming on leaps and bounds. He is eating 3 meals a day plus snacks, they are small meals but it is a massive improvement in where we were a week ago. His spirits are up and he is back to fighting now. The exercises are coming along nicely and we are mentally preparing ourselves for what is next. My sister in law is visiting today which will be lovely for us both but especially Graham so he can have a face to face catch up with his sister for the first time since this bastard disease came into our lives. It is going to be a good day with bacon rolls in the garden, chatting and sunshine. Who can ask for more? Well I could ask that this was all a horrible dream or a mistake and when Graham goes for his scan for them to say T0 N0 M0.

But let's be realistic and let them say that treatment has gone beyond their expectations and now let's cut this bastard out so we get no reoccurrence.

Graham is doing great now, we had a busy day yesterday. I called our nurse to ask whether they wanted him to have the flu jab and after a lovely chat she said flu jab and Covid booster by the end of the month would be great, so flu jabs are booked for Friday 15th and Covid jab bookings open on the 19th for the immunosuppressed so I will book that online. I was also told that his operation was scheduled for early October but it has been pushed back because ICU and anaesthetists are going on strike so it is now scheduled for Monday the 23rd, all being well with the scan results. Not sure if I feel physically sick from relief or terror now we have a date to be honest.
Graham also had a call from the dietitian who is very pleased with him and said to just graze if he cannot manage a big meal, she wants him to put on a bit more weight because he will lose quite a bit after the op but nothing that isn't within our reach to achieve. His exercising is going great and he is getting himself ready for this next battle. Ideally we would like him to tip 12 stone before the op and he is currently just over 12 and a half so is it achievable.
We are off for eye tests this morning which is an hour walking round trip so that will set us up for the day and the weather is continuing to be nice so more time relaxing in the garden too.

It has been a great few days, Graham has been grazing on food nicely, exercising well and generally being a trooper. We are looking after my friends lovely little yorkie for a few days which has done us both the world of good.

We have been playing with her in the garden and it is nice to focus on something other than cancer for a change. He has just eaten a plate of cold meats, some grapes and a dairy Lea dunker pot. I have made him a fruit packed smoothie for later, it is so lovely seeing him eating normally and being himself. We are aware that life will massively change again after the op but that will be taken one day at a time, slowly slowly. It is a case now of, if he fancies something I will make it, when he wants to eat he eats. No pressure, no big plates. This morning he woke up feeling great and said I really fancy a fish finger roll with mayonnaise so we walked to co op to pick up some soft fresh rolls and some fish fingers.
He ate 4 fish fingers and most of the bread roll so it is a fantastic start to the day and it's only 9am. He is going on the exercise bike later and then a nice day in the garden as it is going to be a lovely sunny day and tomorrow looks like a total washout so we are going to make the most of it.

Now is a funny time because nothing is happening, we just pray that the treatment has worked and the op is still on the table. I was going through the freezer looking at what is in there for meals and thinking that we only have 5 weeks of normal eating until our world changes again. Thinking about things he can or cannot take into hospital with him, wondering what he will be eating when he gets home, wondering how long he will be in hospital for, praying that they get every single piece of cancer out, wondering how his recovery will be, praying that they have no complications and hoping with all my heart that he copes well with all this and continues after the op to be the trooper that he has proved to me he can be.

So it is happy 51st birthday to me and scan day today, we will not find anything out today but it will be odd for Graham going back to the hospital again after this few weeks gap, it is like going to visit an old friend in a weird way. Now his life is in the hands again of the big meeting next Tuesday so we can do nothing but wait until we are called in, just like sitting outside the headmasters office not knowing if you are going in for a hiding or to be told that you are going to be made prefect.

Today is The Royal Surrey open day so we are off to see the Da Vinci robot.
Well that was emotional but very interesting, Graham got chatting to a robotic surgeon who was very informative and reassuring while I was talking to a nurse about what will happen when it is op day. She was explaining that he will have nurses around him who change the instruments on the robot arms and assist the surgeon. I actually did feel better that we had seen it in the flesh so to speak but it was very overwhelming at the same time. The one thing that I still feel though is that he truly has the best team looking after him and I am confident that everything will be done to get him through this surgery and out the other side, hopefully cancer free too! We had a great day and Graham is now eating what he wants and his appetite is fantastic, he put on 2lb this week so it is all looking great for surgery as long as his CT scan from last week is looking good. I am hoping that they do not have to do another laparoscopy or anything invasive but if it needs to be done then so be it. In an ideal world, we will get a call on Tuesday to say that the CT clearly shows the cancer has shrunk so much that we cannot see it so it is operation time but I am also realistic that it may not of totally gone to plan. It is just a waiting game now.

In the meantime we have Covid boosters tomorrow as the team said that they would like him to get it because if he gets Covid, it could make him extremely poorly because his immune system is compromised and because they have to collapse a lung during surgery.

We had our Covid vaccines and Graham had no effects at all from it which is the same as all the others, I on the other hand feel like I have been hit by a bus. I fell asleep in the garden after not sleeping last night and Graham came out to see if I fancied fish and chips for lunch as he was going to walk round and pick some up so he is feeling really good bless him.
Today he has had the appetite of an elephant which is fantastic. Surely this must be a good sign, right?

Today was phone call day …….. the tumour has significantly shrunk ! No further tests needed other than the bike test just to test his strength again. No endoscopies, no staging lap, no pet scan, nothing! The relief is amazing! I know we are about to go into a huge battle, I know that on the day of the operation I will be beside myself, I know that there are still risks, I know that there is a 40% chance of a complication and yes I know recovery will be extremely hard BUT the bastard has shrunk, the team were right and this is our only chance of getting this cured ONCE AND FOR ALL! We had a zoom meeting with an anaesthetist which was really informative and helpful, he even shared his screen with us and showed us a video of a patient walking along the corridor a day after having had an oesophogectomy by open surgery. I cannot wait to take a video of Graham doing the same thing. It did show quite how many drains, drips and equipment that will be attached to him post op which looked quite scary.

But it all made sense and of course, they are all there for a reason. He will have more tubes coming out of him than the London Underground but they slowly get taken out as the days go by and the recovery process begins. He will be admitted at 6pm on Sunday the 22nd of October and all necessary pre op tests and preparation will be done that night ready for him to go straight to theatre at 7.30am the following day. If it all goes to plan it will take 10 hours but can take longer.

Graham did ask if he could go back to work for the 3 weeks that we have left before his op and the nurse said he could but he must not catch Covid so we weighed up the pros and cons, pros are he will gain strength and stamina which will help for the op, better mental health by getting out of the house and having some normality and the only con is Covid which would delay his op if he caught it so we are thinking hard about what to do. On one hand he could catch Covid going for his bike test at the hospital or walking in a shop but on the other hand he has got more chance catching it going into pubs and restaurants in London. We are going to call his boss today to see if a plan can be made and what is best to do. We decided to get out for some fresh air so we walked in and saw Grahams boss who was so chuffed to see him and we all decided that he will go back to work on Monday for the next 3 weeks to help him get as fit as he can for his op. He will be on light duties but every bit of exercise will help him. We have ordered him some decent masks and checked his hand sanitiser so it is like the start of the Covid pandemic once again but we have to protect my boy as we have come this far and we just cannot have his operation delayed. I need robocop to do its thing and get this bastard cancer out once and for all. I have learnt that we are such a strong couple and we will beat this. I know that now.

I have to because I am done crying and being emotional and I do know with all my heart that we will be the Keyworth dream team once again.

It is amazing to think that from diagnosis to the operation date is only 23 weeks and 4 days which is fantastic and a great accolade to the NHS. He has had scans, an operation, chemo, radiotherapy, various tests and a rest period in that time. I have been able to go back to my happy place today for the first time in months, I made a puffball bread, a loaf of bread, eggs Royale for breakfast and a rotisserie pork joint with Pomme Anna potatoes for dinner.
Life is actually quite normal and will be up until Graham goes into hospital on the 22nd so we are making the most of it as we will be back to square one again very soon. Today I will be cooking homemade pizzas in the wood fired oven which is Grahams favourite. It is sort of surreal really, Graham is looking and feeling great so it seems odd that we will be taking him back to hospital to be battered. Can't it all just go away and let us carry on with our normal life.

We met our fantastic surgeon today, He went through the procedure explaining that the stomach part of the operation should take roughly 4 hours with the remaining 6 hours on the oesophagus. He explained that there is a 5% chance of death nationally although at our hospital it is lower. There is also a risk of a stroke, heart attack and a 50% chance of any complications which could be a number of things but it is things like a leak from the join where the stomach is joined to the oesophagus. He said that Graham is very low risk as he is so fit and he explained that he has a team of 4 registrars and himself to look after Graham.

He said that if anything goes wrong he will fix it. They are also looking at no feeding tube being needed but if things change and they feel that it could be beneficial, they can put one in at any time. He said he is hoping that Graham should be home between 6 and 9 days, all being well. Becky, our GI nurse was also there and she told us that Graham scored exactly the same on his exercise bike test last week as he did prior to treatment which is astonishing. The surgeon said that Graham is in the 1% of people who have done that. He is very confident that Graham has the best chance of getting through this and was extremely reassuring that he and his team are completely confident in what is to come. We were told that Graham will no longer feel hungry after the operation as part of what they remove controls you feeling hungry and that he also will never have that empty rumbling stomach feeling as there is no big empty stomach to give him that sensation so he will have to remember to eat little and often each day to get sufficient calories and nutrients. I was just saying to Graham that I am so chuffed at how lovely our surgeon seemed and that I am happy that he is in charge of Robocops joysticks but Graham said, no it's Robodoc ! So now it is Robodoc that is going to save my boy.

We have just got back from our final pre surgery meeting which was his pre op and physio assessment. The pre op was blood taken, oximeter, blood pressure, weight and MRSA test, he was given a pack to bring home which is a nasal ointment to be applied to each nostril 3 times a day for 5 days and a skin and hair wash to use each day. We then went to see our physio Rachel who chatted about the operation and post op exercises, explaining that ICU has its own dedicated physios who will be working with Graham to get him walking more each day.

He will be starting with two lots of walking on day one after the operation and increasing each day. She briefly spoke about breathing exercises which is extremely important to get his lungs back to normal and inflating well. She then explained that she was going to do the 3 tests on him that they did pre treatment just to see how he is doing and not expecting him to do any better because of the toll that chemo radio takes, she said if it is the same that would be great. So first up was the 6 minute walking test, followed by a grip test and finally the sit to standing in 1 minute. Well he smashed it ! Walking was a lot more than pre treatment, grip was better too and sit to standing was 2 more.

She was so proud of him at how extremely well he has done and said it was more than she could hope for. She said I am working next week so I will pop into ICU and see how you are doing which was lovely of her. The entire team feel like friends now as they have gone through this with us from the start.

Admittance day has come, it is the 22nd of October. Graham has his bag packed and is just waiting for his lift. I am trying to hold it together and we are both happy with the decision that he is going in on his own as I will really upset him if I go and have to leave him. He is still so positive while I keep looking at him thinking is this the last time I ever see him, will he ever come home, what if…

The time came and Graham said see you on Tuesday and then he kissed me, I had to use all my strength to not beg him to not go and just stay with me. As soon as he walked out the door I broke down and had a feeling of utter terror. I felt lost, lonely and scared.

Our friend Shirley had come round with her husband Don who took Graham off and Shirley came to see me, it was great timing as she calmed me down, changed the subject and was such a great help. Graham was texting telling us that he had his own room and was settling in, he had his blood pressure and bloods taken and from what he said, they were starting his prep already and really looking after him. I had a few beers thinking it would help me sleep but that backfired as I went to bed at midnight and was wide awake at 3am with a lump in my throat and a feeling of utter panic and dread. Graham text me in the morning and was still in high spirits even though he was about to face a 10 hour op. He went off for a shower and put his gown on, had a visit from one of the surgeons and then the anaesthetist who went through the op with him again and said that he would be going down between 8 and 8.15am so he put on his compression socks and text me saying love you loads, speak to you soon. I replied and said do you promise and he said yes. Graham never breaks a promise so he had better not bloody break this one.

Can I just tell you that no one can prepare you for the wait, the anxiety, the living nightmare day that happens. I felt sick, I cried, I felt dread, I cried, I felt helpless, I cried, I felt lost and just in case you didn't get the gist, I cried. You count down every single hour. I was thinking at hour 9 do not have a stroke or heart attack now, you are nearly there, come on Graham you have got this. It got to 7.30pm and my nerves got the better of me so I called ICU. They were so lovely as soon as I explained that I was just so worried, the nurse said don't worry, let me find out. She put me on hold for a minute and said I will be right back.

I know she had gone off to find out any news but it felt like I was holding on for ages so I started thinking what if something has gone wrong, what if he is still in surgery, oh my god what if he is …… No stop those thoughts right now. But what if she is finding someone to come and tell me the bad news. Then I heard her lovely cheerful voice say he is in recovery and he will be with them in 45 minutes. The relief was amazing, I shook from emotion. At 8.30pm one of the surgeons called me and said Graham is very tired but it all went to plan and he is safely in ICU. I thanked her so much and burst into tears on the phone. I messaged family and friends with tears rolling down my face. I have never in my 51 years had such an emotionally draining day. I did keep myself busy but there is nothing or no one that can take your mind off of it.

I can visit him from tomorrow which I cannot wait for but in the meantime, I need some sleep and to start eating properly as I will need to be on top of my game to help Graham recover.
Well that never happened as I was getting messages from everyone who were obviously very concerned so I eventually went to bed at just before midnight and was wide awake by 3am again thinking is he ok, did he have a good night, were there any complications. I called icu at 8am and they said that he had a good night but didn't sleep very well although absolutely nothing to worry about and it is to be expected. The main thing is that all his vitals are good. 1 night behind him now which must be a good sign.

Walking towards the doors that say Intensive Care Unit is actually quite daunting but I felt strong as I had received my first message from Graham saying that he felt ok and that he was looking forward to seeing me.

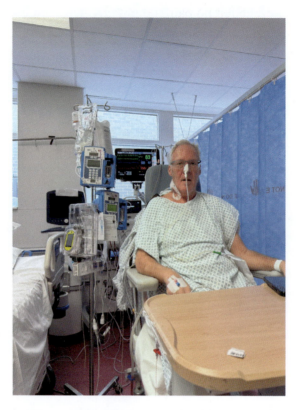

I knew what to expect in as much as drainage tubes and various other contraptions. But let me tell you, nothing prepares you for seeing your loved one looking so utterly vulnerable and broken. Don't get me wrong, underneath the stomach drain that was taped to his nose and looking past all the equipment, he actually looked really good but my emotions got the better of me and I did have a little cry which then upset him which was the last thing I wanted to do but we soon got over that and started chatting.
He was a little bit out of it from the anaesthetic and pain meds and looked very tired but other than that, he was great. The nurses are amazing, checking constantly and being so caring and vigilant.

Graham said he felt no pain and was allowed 50ml of water every hour. The surgeons had been to see him and explained that they are very happy with how the operation went. He also had a visit from the physio who went through exercises with him to help his lungs and also to get him on his feet, they even had him walking. I had been with Graham about an hour when he said to the nurse, it's time for your walk which filled me with excitement but also trepidation. What if he falls, what if he passes out, what if he pulls one of the many tubes out. Three nurses flanked him, one either side to carry his drains and one at the back to push his chair behind him in case he felt dizzy and had to sit down. Then they said ok Graham ready when you are, nice and steady. Graham stood straight up with such confidence it was outstanding then he casually started walked along with the nurses at his pace. I went ahead to start recording him coming towards me on my phone which was such a fantastic site, I had gone around a corner and seeing him appear just filled me with such pride and admiration.

After settling him back down in his chair we chatted about what I had been doing and all the tests and checks he has been having but after 2 hours he looked absolutely shattered and almost asleep sitting up so I said why don't you go to bed but he said no it's too early and sitting up for as long as I can will help my lungs so he knows exactly what is going on and what he needs to do.

I went home so happy that I knew he was going to be ok and certainly was being cared for amazingly. I ate my first meal in a couple of days and slept soundly which resulted in me waking up feeling ready for the next chapter. My husband, best friend, soul mate is a Warrior !

Day 2 and Graham is doing great. He had a little blip when his blood pressure dropped but the nurses raised his legs and gave him an IV bag of fluid which sorted him out and he remained stable. The surgeon wasn't at all concerned and said it can happen but it is fine. When I was visiting his blood oxygen dropped to 83 which made me panic but the nurse was so calm and said to Graham keep your hand still and I watched it start gaining again until it reached 98. The oximeter is so sensitive that if it moves even slightly, it starts dropping but soon stabilises again. The main thing is that the surgeons and doctor are extremely pleased to the point that the nurses were told that he could have one of his drains taken out. Graham said the pain was excruciating when they removed it from his side so they gave him an extra shot of morphine which soon got him comfortable. Then he had to have a chest X-ray at 9pm which is all routine and is done in the ICU at his bed. The poor bugger was so shattered when I saw him as he isn't sleeping well with the bright lights and noises around him but I am hoping that after todays morphine and lots going on that he will finally rest and sleep well tonight.

It is Thursday the 26th of October and Graham had a great nights sleep, he is just left with one chest drain, catheter, epidural, and the 3 tubes in his neck for meds and fluids. He has been told by his nurse that he is ready for soup, tea and jelly and that he is ready to go onto a ward after only 3 days which is absolutely amazing ! He was in such great spirits when I visited, he had a shave and looked great now without the stomach drain. My Graham was starting to come back.

A pain management lady came and explained that the medication will be different on the ward as it is a step towards going home.

The dietician had also been and given Graham a leaflet explaining that when he comes home it will be 14 days of puréed food followed by 2-4 months of minced and moist building up to normal textures. He is to eat 6 times a day with portions no bigger than his palm which we both think is manageable and we will adapt. I am truly astounded at his progress. He was not lucky to get cancer and he is not lucky to have a life altering operation but bugger me, he is coming home and that is all that matters.

The surgeons are very happy, the doctors are very happy and I am very happy. He has progressed today from water to a cup of tea, apple juice, orange juice, soup and jelly. God he makes me so proud. I left him at 4 as he was going for another walk and then have his dinner (yes dinner! Not 50ml of water every hour) an actual meal, followed by a doctors visit to check that he is ok and give him a blood thinning injection to help avoid clotting and deep vein thrombosis. We have done our usual chatting via messenger until he gets tired. He said that there are no beds in the ward so he is staying where he is tonight which is fine as he gets one on one nursing and I am happy that he is being monitored after eating for the first time since the operation.

The surgeon said to Graham that he is superhuman because he is at the stage that he would expect on day 10 after the op not on day 4! He is still in ICU as no beds on the ward but that is fine as he gets so much great care. He is amusing the nurses and getting stronger each day considering his insides have been totally messed around with.

Day 5 and Graham is doing so well, he is on the ward now. His epidural has been removed and it is puréed food day which is a great step on the way to recovery. He has made friends with a couple of the guys on the ward which is nice and passes the time by chatting and going for walks with one of the guys. He had a puréed casserole which he said was quite nice and went down a treat.

Graham is getter better each day, he had his last chest drain and central lines which come out of his neck removed today. This is all in preparation for tomorrows discharge day. The surgeon is still very happy with him and his vitals are all great. We know this will be a long recovery but we are both ready for it and looking forward to him being cancer free once and for all and him coming home and being comfortable in his home surroundings.

Today, Monday 30th of October was discharge day so I went to the hospital at 3pm for the last hour of visiting and then hang around until he was ready to go. Our nurse came round and told us that his inflammation markers in his blood had gone up to 102 but everything else was good so she needed a word with the surgeon. At 4.30pm the surgeon came to see us and said it is nothing to worry about but it could be inflammation from the internal trauma, it could be an infection or it could be a leak so to be on the safe side they are keeping Graham in another 24 hours and will re do the blood test tomorrow. It was so disheartening as he has done so amazingly well but we both know it is for the best and we are happy that neither of us want Graham home until they are happy and sure he is ok. The last thing we want is to be calling 999 in the middle of the night if he has a problem.

It's 12.40pm on Halloween and I have just received a message from Graham saying that the nurse has seen his blood results and the markers have gone down. He is going to chat with the surgeon to get it moving so that we are good to go. I think my boy is coming home!
We have had the good to go chat. Just waiting for his medication, quick lesson in how to inject blood thinners for 28 days and then he can come home. I honestly cannot wait until I look next to me on the sofa and there he is. I cannot wait until he is annoying me asking me for things, I just cannot wait until my boy is back.

I arrived at the hospital at 4.30pm and Graham looked absolutely shattered, he was ready to come home and get some much needed sleep. At 5.30 the nurse came in with 2 bags of medication and went through each one so we were happy with what needed taking when. He asked me to give Graham his blood thinning injection under supervision to make sure I was ok with it. Well I certainly didn't realise quite how sharp the needles were so I was a bit over zealous and it went in so deep that the actual needle went all the way in and I hit his thigh with the shaft so I now know that it needs the gentlest of pushes. By day 28 I will have probably got the hang of it and that is when we finish them. The medication is not too bad to get your head around, he has multi vitamins & minerals, the blood thinning injections, paracetamol, codeine phosphate, lansoprazole, laxatives because of the codeine and mouthwash until the bottle is empty. We arrived home at roughly 6.30pm, quickly opened up the medication bags and got out the paracetamol and codeine for Graham to take before he went to bed for the first nights quiet, dark and peaceful sleep in over a week.

Day one of having my Graham back, I am making salmon mousse, mackerel mousse and puréed fish pie today for the next day or 2 and enough for the freezer to try and give Graham some variety from soups and puréed meat dishes. He woke up feeling great and got some much needed sleep.

We have booked a nurses appointment at our local doctors surgery for Tuesday the 7th to have his staples removed from the 3 wounds in his back and we should also get an appointment to go and see our surgeon to discuss histology results from the operation in 2 weeks or so. He has 6 little holes on his front from the robot that are tiny and are glued so they are no problem at all but his back has one wound with 2 staples in it where his chest drain was, one underneath with 3 staples from the robot and then a larger one with 9 staples that I think was from the lung and oesophagus part of the op.

Graham was feeling great but had pain where his staples are so he called the GP who swapped the codeine phosphate for Tramadol which hopefully will work and also he will be much less likely to feel rough from the codeine as he did when he was on co codamol as I am sure you remember from earlier in this story at the start of this journey. He is eating so well and is feeling hungry which is fantastic. God I admire his strength, he genuinely is my hero. Yes, you read it right he is feeling hungry !

We have had our letter to meet with our surgeon on Tuesday the 14th which will be 2 weeks to the day from Grahams discharge. The Tramadol is working so now he is in no pain, eating great and feeling great.

Graham is still extremely positive about getting fit and strong again ready for his immunotherapy and to get back to a normal as can be life. Do not get me wrong, everyone's story is different and it is an extremely hard time to go through. Will life ever be the same again … No. Will your relationship go through stresses and strains … Yes. Will they beat cancer … who knows. Will you find out who your friends are … Yes. Will you want to throw in the towel and want to scream … yes. Will you cry, scream, feel useless, feel utterly deflated … yes. Will you get through this and never stop loving them … Fuck Yes!

I grieved for our relationship, I grieve for Grahams health, both of which I had always taken for granted. I am so hugely proud of what his body has been through yet here he stands. I am so hugely proud that our marriage and love for each other is as strong as it was on our wedding day. It's tough but take time for yourself and look after yourself and your loved one and you will get through it. Scarred, battered and frightened but healing with time and patience.

It is D Day, Tuesday the 14th of November and we have been to see our surgeon. I was convinced he would say he had taken out x amount of lymph nodes and unfortunately they were all cancerous, sorry but it is bad news, sadly it is not looking good. But ….. he actually said I removed 47 lymph nodes and the histology report shows that not a single one showed any sign of cancer ! Not 1! You are now officially T1 N0 M0. So from stage 3 with it in at least 2 lymph nodes but no spread, Graham is now Stage 1 in no lymph nodes and no spread so the chemotherapy and radiotherapy along with surgery has worked. The relief is amazing, I am so happy and now we have massive hope for the future.

We will have a meeting with our oncologist to confirm immunotherapy and a follow up with our surgeon in 3 months. He said he is so happy at how well Graham is doing and to just keep on exercising, eating well and building his strength up. I am aware that not everyone is luckily enough to have Robodoc and not everyone's recovery is as good or as quick. It is hard to think that Graham still has had major surgery and although his scars are less than traditional open surgery, he still has been through the mill and he still has had life changing surgery and recovery will take time. I look at him and think he is back to normal forgetting that actually his insides are working like the clappers to work out what is different and to adjust to his new interior design.

We were just looking at Grahams scars that are healing very nicely, the 6 holes on his front have almost gone and the ones on his back are looking great, even the big one has settled down lovely. They will always be a constant reminder of his battle but we look upon them as a positive that they show what he has been through and that cancer doesn't always win. He has been lucky to have no infections in any of them and we are aware that not everyone is that lucky. There can be so many setbacks along the way sadly. It is not always plain sailing and it can add the the stress of an already shitty situation but we have to take every positive that we can.

Graham is managing to eat well as long as it is something in a sauce which is so much better than the start of this nightmare. It will be a few months until he is ready for normal textures but the end is in sight and finally the light at the end of the tunnel does not feel like it is the train coming the other way. We know how far he has come.

He is eating curries, yoghurt, stews, casseroles, soft desserts and anything that slides down easily. We are hoping that he may even manage a Christmas dinner albeit a small one so that is our goal and we have just over 5 weeks of healing to go so fingers crossed that he will manage it.

Our days are getting easier, the tiredness is subsiding for Graham and he is now looking forward to when he can go back to work and normal life can start again. It is like we have been pressing pause and then play and then pause again. At the moment we are in slow motion working towards full speed. Christmas is my favourite time of year usually but I just cannot get my head around it yet. Normally by now I have a box in the shed that starts getting filled up with non perishable food goodies, I am buying presents and hiding them away and I start thinking it won't be long until the decorations go up and everything looks pretty. This year it all just seems so insignificant somehow. Don't get me wrong, I will get there and we will have a great Christmas being together under the twinkly lights but at the moment I am just grateful that he is here.

Graham is nearly 4 weeks post op and today he has tried a beef casserole with mash and it went down well, he was apprehensive because he thought it didn't break up enough when he chewed it but that is a mind over matter thing as it was fine but I totally understand as he has had to be so careful for months and that will take some getting over. He had toast as well today with some boiled eggs for breakfast which surprisingly he had no problems with either. We are praying that this means he is healing and hopefully won't need any stretches doing and that food will be ok. It is baby steps though.

We are fully aware that it will be some weeks until he can eat totally normal textures but each thing he tries and manages is a great achievement. He went off for a walk this morning too which was the first one on his own. I did worry a bit wondering if he was ok or if he slipped on wet leaves of which there are so many about at the moment but he came back happy that he had stretched his legs and got some fresh air in his lungs without me which probably did him good and gave him time to think about things and get lost in his own thoughts.

We are nearly 5 weeks post op now and food is going well, we are trying to keep up with small amounts every couple of hours and adding more calories into each meal because when Graham weighed himself last Sunday, he had dropped to 11 stone 1 which is a stone less than when he went in for his op so we are desperately trying to build him back up now. He has been having a supplement drink each day along with soups, jacket potatoes with lots of butter, desserts, fish in creamy sauces, ready brek, and minced meat. We will see what Sunday brings but hopefully we will see a slight increase each week now until he finds his new normal. Graham is doing well on getting his fitness back too, he is walking each day and using his exercise bike so slowly he will regain strength and muscle ready to start working again which he is desperate to do.

I am off over the allotment today which gives us both a break from each other. We have acquired a shed so it is base levelling, edging and weeding on the cards. We are lucky that it is supposed to be 12 degrees today which is great considering it is nearly the end of November.

It's funny to think that the year is coming near its end when most of it has been a blur of tests, hospital, operations and worry. I thought the pandemic was bad, well 2023 can seriously do one. 2024 is going to be our year, a year of great health and getting back on track with our lives.

I purchased some protein bars for Graham hoping that they will help but sadly within half an hour of him eating one he had bad stomach ache so we are trying to work out what particular ingredient it was that has done it. Such a shame as they are massive in protein but if his new plumbing says no then no it is. This is going to be such a learning curve to see what his system agrees and disagrees with. Today has been great though as Graham had ready brek with Manuka honey, some biscuits, chicken soup, the dreaded protein bar and then butter chicken with half a jacket potato with lashings of butter followed by some homemade stollen with custard. The tummy pain did happen before when Graham had bread with soup so we are thinking that it could possibly be that he ate a little too much or it could be a particular ingredient but we will work it out with trial and error.

We had a letter today with our oncologists appointment for next Wednesday the 29th of November so we will find out when immunotherapy starts. We have been told it is an injection every 4 weeks for a year and that it will be a slog but if it means that this bastard never returns then it will all be worth it. Graham is still very determined so I am sure he will face it head on as he has done with everything else so far.

Today we went to see our oncologist who explained that the chemotherapy and radiotherapy combined had done such a good that the tumour was very small when the operation was done and because the histology came back with all 47 lymph nodes being clear, all cancer has gone! Yep you heard that right. ALL CANCER HAS GONE.

We decided that now we have come this far, it was time to put the news on social media. I posted a video of Grahams walk the day after surgery and explained briefly what we have been through, concluding that the cancer has gone. We had lovely comments and support from friends and the video on Instagram has had over 5000 views so far which is fantastic and just shows what can be done the day after life altering major surgery so I hope it inspires others. It's funny as we have now shared our story, there is an almost sense of relief that it isn't a secret anymore and people can ask us whatever they want because we are both strong enough now to talk about it and hopefully help others.

Graham will now start a year of immunotherapy which will be an intravenous drip every 4 weeks but it is his best chance of our unwelcome visitor not coming back into our lives so we are more than happy to start our next journey.

We had a phone call today informing us that the first immunotherapy infusion of Nivolumab will be Friday the 8th of December in the same place that Graham had his chemo so we are both familiar with where it will be. I have been reading through the side effects, not to worry myself but more to be aware of what to look out for. We will be going back to checking Grahams temperature regularly and keeping him as fit as we can.

We get another cancer card or patient alert card as it is called which will be taken with Graham wherever he goes as it will have to be shown to any doctor or healthcare professional should the need arise. We will also have the 24 hour/7 days a week helpline again in case we have any questions or concerns which really does help because sometimes things crop up and it is great to know that someone is always on the end of the phone.

Graham has also decided that he is ready to go back to work! Not lifting heavy crates all day but chauffeuring a person who will do the lifting, he can then start getting his strength back slowly until he feels ready to start doing it on his own again. His recovery is truly remarkable considering 6 weeks ago he was undergoing an 11 hour operation. I truly do admire his courage and determination. We need for him to gain a little weight and strength and he feels that going back to normal life and work will help, which I agree with him wholeheartedly. Let's get our life back again and remind cancer that it has lost its battle and to never darken our door again.

Today was immunotherapy number 1 and we arrived at the department ready to see how this new lot of drugs drugs would affect Graham. He went into the familiar room to get his vitals checked while I wandered off to the lounge area for a coffee. I looked around and all you can see is scared, frightened and worried patients and relatives. There is a sense of calm in the room but also absolute terror. I took my coffee back to Graham and looked at him hooked up to the familiar bag of wonder drugs ready for his infusion.

Half an hour later and it was all done, no reactions thank god and Graham was his usual jokey self talking to the nurses and having a laugh with them as though it was just a normal day.

We are aware that he can get side effects at anytime but that is a hurdle to cross if we have to.

A heartfelt thank you to anyone who has taken the time to read this. I am sorry if I bored you in parts but I hope you can take something away from it and if it has helped even in the tiniest way then I am truly humbled and happy.

Our journey is not finished by a long chalk but for now we are counting our blessings, looking forward to the future and just being together.

Shoutout to all you Warriors and Carers. You are all AMAZING and don't ever forget it.

Graham with his best mate Robodoc

Special thanks to Don & Shirley for tirelessly taking us to numerous appointments, for the emotional support and for being great friends and bloody great human beings. Pari for listening to me daily and supporting us even though she lost her soulmate and husband to bastard cancer but was still there for us at every step. Both of our families for going through this with us and never making us feel like we were alone.

Remember, Must be strong for him.

CANCER 0 - KEYWORTH 1 so far ... ...

Printed in Great Britain
by Amazon